AF584760

WESTERN AUSTRALIA

First published in 2025 by New Holland Publishers
Sydney, Australia.
newhollandpublishers.com

 A record of this book is held at the National Library of Australia.

ISBN: 9781760797829

Managing Director: Fiona Schultz
General Manager/Publisher: Olga Dementiev
Designer: Andrew Davies
Production Director: Arlene Gippert
Printed in China

WESTERN AUSTRALIA

RioTinto
LAVAN

ERECTED
BY GRATEFUL CITIZENS
IN REMEMBRANCE OF
MEN OF THIS STATE
WHO AT THE CALL OF DUTY
GAVE THEIR LIVES FOR
FREEDOM AND HUMANITY
IN
THE GREAT WAR
1914 - 1918

Rio Tinto
LAVAN

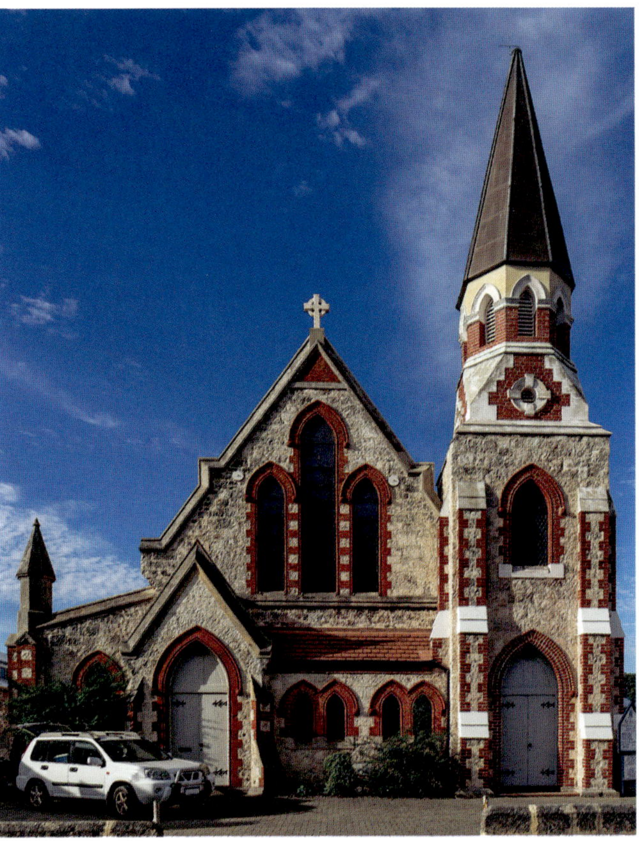

V R
1855

G
H
E
F
N°1 DIVISION

F

TEA ROOMS

you're welcome
at St John's
our church is open for you
every day for quiet time
every Sunday 9.00am

KALGOORLIE
ROADS BOARD
CHAMBERS

50

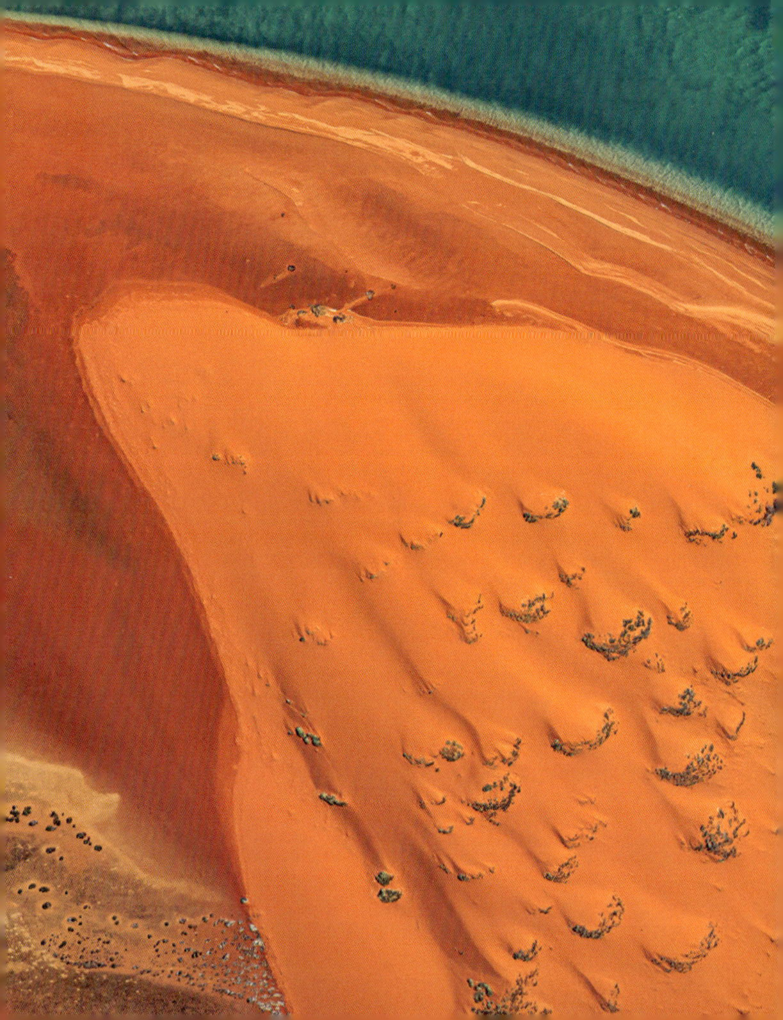

WESTERN AUSTRALIA

- Western Australia covers **one third** of the land of Australia and is the biggest state in Australia.
- Perth's nickname is '**The City of Lights**' but also the wildflower state.
- Western Australia has over **12,500 kilometres** of coastline.
- **Perth** is situated on the west coast of the Australian continent in south-west Western Australia and faces west to the Indian Ocean.
- Perth is famous for being the most isolated city in the world, with its closest city being Adelaide, over **2,600 kilometres** away.
- A nickname of a Western Australian local is called a '**Sandgroper**'.
- Just over **10%** of the Australian population live in Western Australia; and of those people 80% of the population live in Perth.

- Western Australia is home to **Lucky Bay** and the country's whitest beach.
- **Busselton Jetty** is the longest Wooden Jetty in the Southern Hemisphere stretching 1.8 kilometres and takes 25 minutes to walk each way with an underwater observatory at the end of the jetty.
- **Kings Park** covers 400 hectares and ranks as one of the world's largest urban parks in a city.
- The **Margaret River** region is one of the best places in Western Australia to explore caves.
- The **Nullarbor Plain** stretches over millions of hectares across Western Australia.
- **The Pinnacles** are limestone pillars formed around 25,000 to 30,000 years ago within the Nambung National Park.
- The **Wave Rock** was formed by weathering and water erosion millions of years ago.
- Western Australia has **pink lakes**.
- The world's happiest animal lives in Western Australia – the **Quokka**. Most of these cute creatures live on Rottnest Island.